HAL•LEONARD

pro vocal®
BETTER THAN KARAOKE!

GREAT STANDARDS COLLECTION

M000160076

ISBN 978-1-4234-8114-0

HAL•LEONARD®
CORPORATION
7777 W. BLUEMOUND RD. P.O. BOX 13819 MILWAUKEE, WI 53213

Visit Hal Leonard Online at
www.halleonard.com

CONTENTS
CD 1

CONTENTS
CD 2

Blue Skies

from BETSY
Words and Music by Irving Berlin

Intro
Freely

Hee, _____ hee - ya - da - da - don - da - da - da -

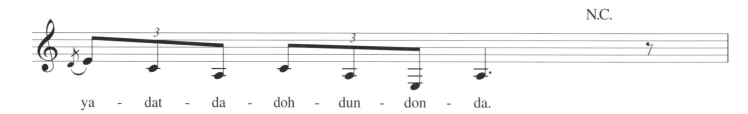

ya - dat - da - doh - dun - don - da.

Ba - ba - do - da - dee - a - doo - ba - dee - ba - doo - ba - doh - bee - yoo - doo - ya.

Da - yee - a - doo - da - weed - ya - doo - da - lee - la - loo - la - yoo - ya -

ya. Ya - la - lo - la - ya.

Chorus
Moderately

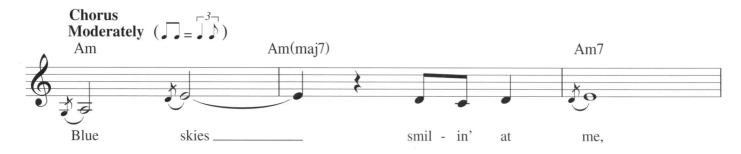

Blue skies _____ smil - in' at me,

- ry - ing by, _____ when _____ you're _ in love, _____ my, _

Chorus

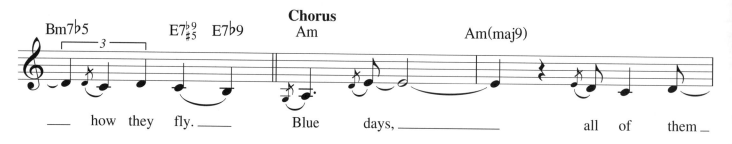

_____ how they fly. _____ Blue days, _____ all of them _

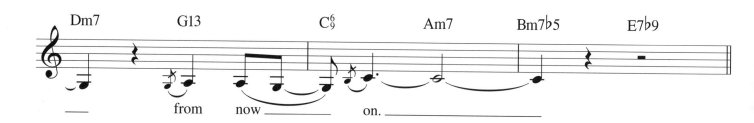

_____ gone, _____ noth - ing but _____ blue _____ skies _____

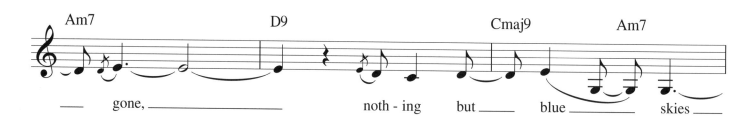

_____ from now _____ on. _____

Interlude

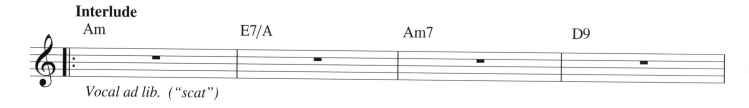

Vocal ad lib. ("scat")

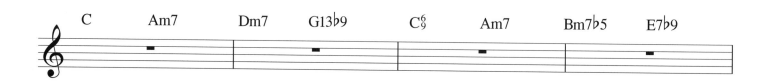

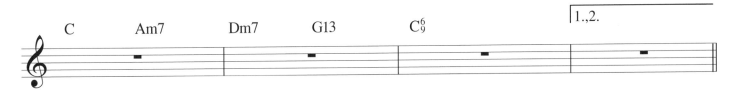

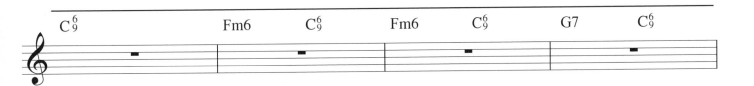

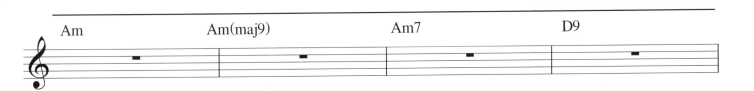

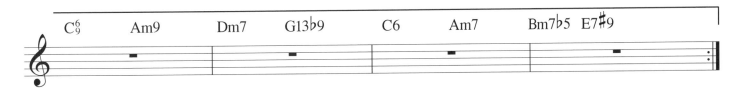

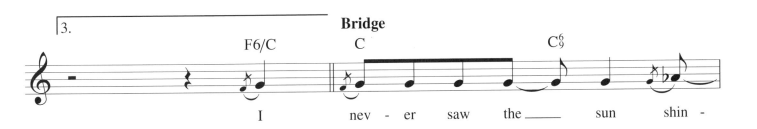

oh, ___ so right. ___ No - tic - ing the days hur -

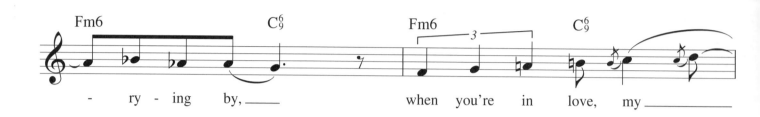

- ry - ing by, ___ when you're in love, my ___

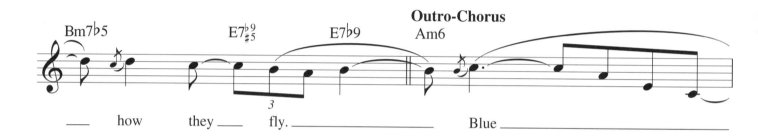

___ how they ___ fly. ___ Blue ___

Outro-Chorus

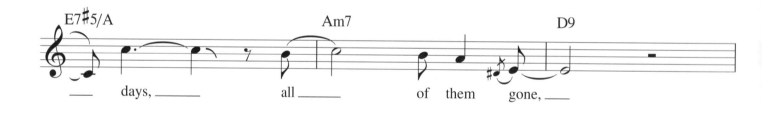

___ days, ___ all ___ of them gone, ___

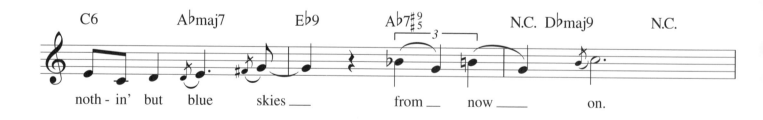

noth - in' but blue skies ___ from ___ now ___ on.

Ba - doo - ba - dee - ya - doop - 'm - boop - 'n - boo - wa. ___

Boogie Woogie Bugle Boy

from BUCK PRIVATES
Words and Music by Don Raye and Hughie Prince

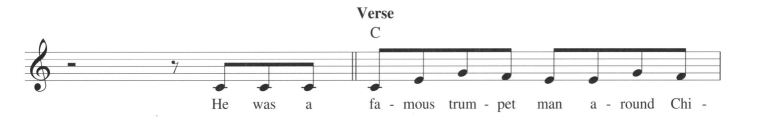

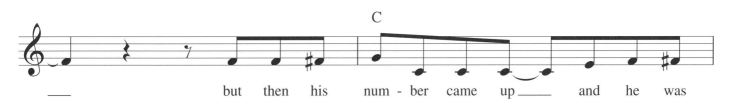

called to the draft. __ He's in the ar - my now, a - blow - in'

rev - eil - le. He's __ the boo - gie woo - gie bu - gle boy of

Verse

Com - pa - ny B. __ They made him blow a bu - gle for his

Un - cle Sam. __ It real - ly brought him down be - cause he

could not jam. __ The cap - tain seemed to un - der - stand, __

__ be - cause the next day the cap' __ went out and

draft - ed the band, __ and now the com - pa - ny jumps when he plays

rev - eil - le. He's __ the boo - gie woo - gie bu - gle boy of

Chorus

C/G — Com - pa - ny B. ____

C — A - root, a - toot, a -

too - dle - i - a - ta toot, he blows it

C7 — eight to the bar ____

in boo - gie rhy - thm. He can't blow a note ___ un - less a

F

bass and gui - tar ____ is play - in' with him,

C7 _____

___ and ____ the com - pa - ny jumps when he plays

G9

rev - eil - le. He's ___ the boo - gie woo - gie bu - gle boy of

F7   C

Com - pa - ny B. ____

Bridge

C   N.C. — He was some boo -

- gie woo - gie bu - gle boy of Com - pa - ny B, _____

Chorus

boo - gie woo - gie bu - gle boy of Com - pa - ny B. _____ A -

Chorus

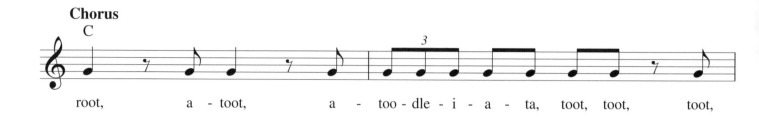

root, a - toot, a - too - dle - i - a - ta, toot, toot, toot,

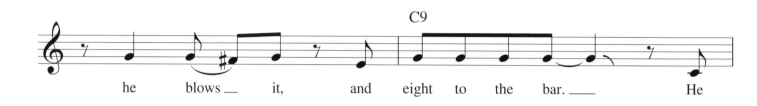

he blows __ it, and eight to the bar. _____ He

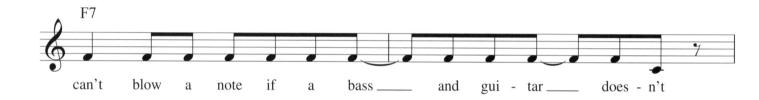

can't blow a note if a bass _____ and gui - tar _____ does - n't

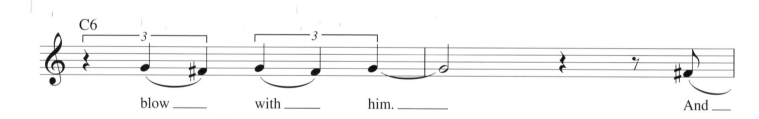

blow _____ with _____ him. _____ And __

__ the com - pa - ny jumps when he plays rev - eil - le. He's __ the

Outro

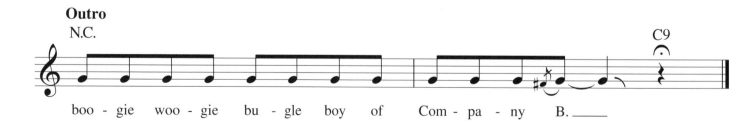

boo - gie woo - gie bu - gle boy of Com - pa - ny B. _____

Cabaret

from the Musical CABARET
Words by Fred Ebb
Music by John Kander

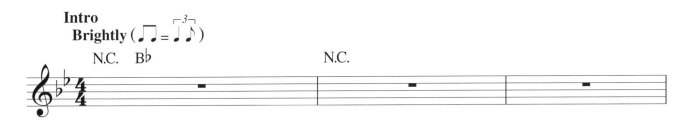

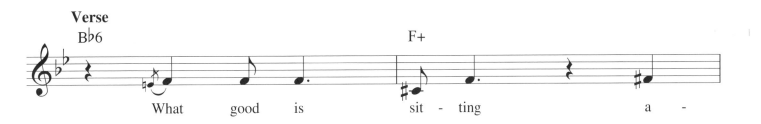

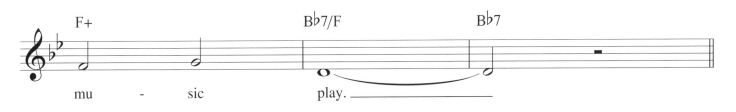

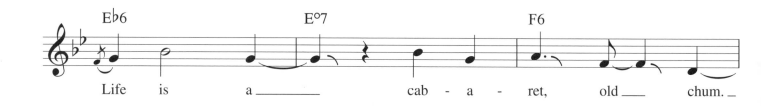

Life is a _____ cab - a - ret, old ___ chum. _

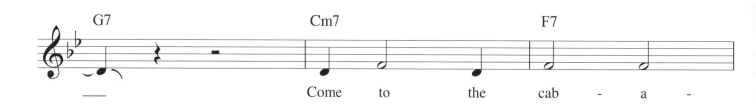

___ Come to the cab - a -

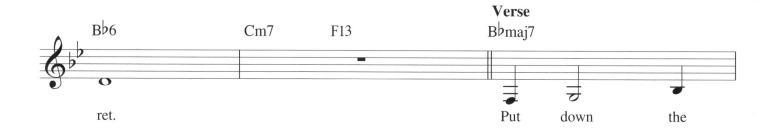

Verse

ret. Put down the

knit - ting, the book and the broom. ____ It's

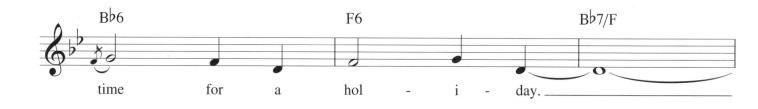

time for a hol - i - day. _____

Chorus

___ Life is a _____ cab - a -

ret, old ___ chum. ___ Come to the

cab - a - ret.
Come taste the wine, ___

Bridge

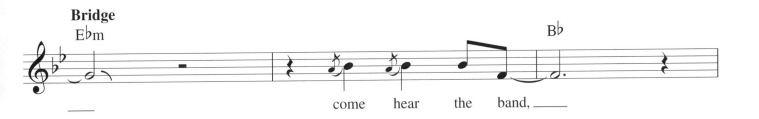

___
come hear the band, ___

come blow your horn, ___ start cel - e - brat - ing.

Right this way your ta - ble's wait - ing.

Verse

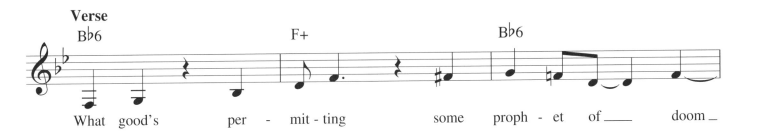

What good's per - mit - ting some proph - et of ___ doom ___

___ to wipe ev - 'ry smile a -

Chorus

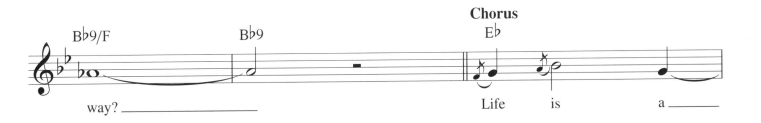

way? _____ Life is a ___

cab - a - ret, old chum, _so_

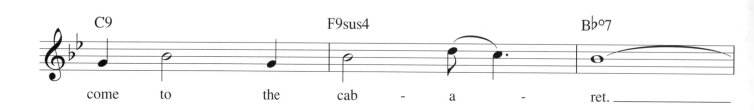

come to the cab - a - ret.

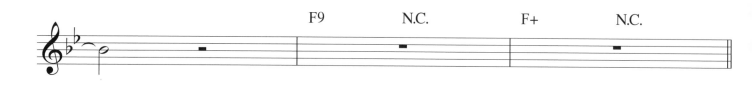

Verse

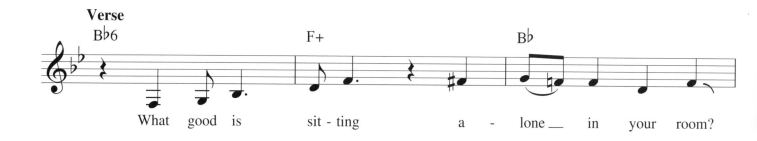

_What good is sit - ting a - lone _ in your room?_

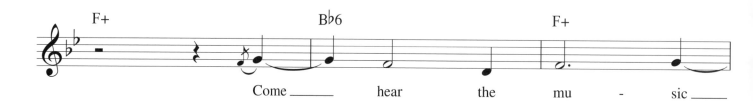

Come _hear the mu - sic_

Chorus

_ play._ _Life is a _

cab - a - ret, old chum.

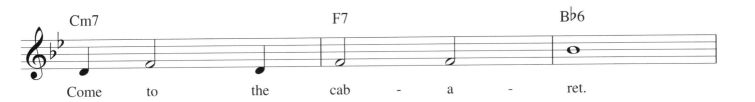

Come to the cab - a - ret.

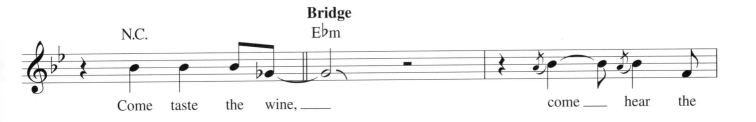

Bridge

Come taste the wine, _____ come _____ hear the

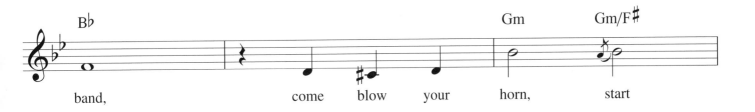

band, come blow your horn, start

cel - e - brat - ing. Right this way, your

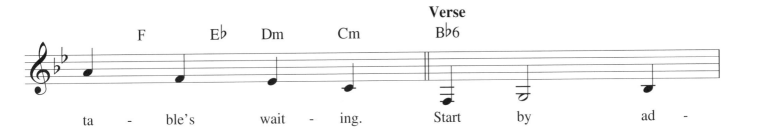

Verse

ta - ble's wait - ing. Start by ad -

mit - ting, from cra - dle to tomb, _____ it

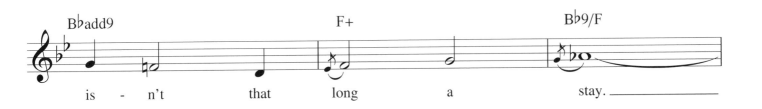

is - n't that long a stay. _____

Outro-Chorus

Life is a _____ cab - a -

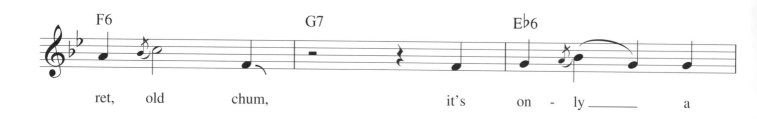

ret, old chum, it's on - ly _____ a

cab - a - ret, old _____ chum, _____ and

I love a cab -

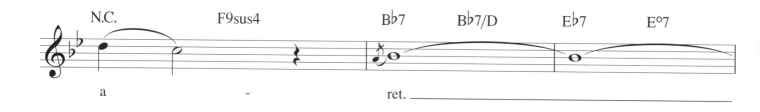

a - ret. _____

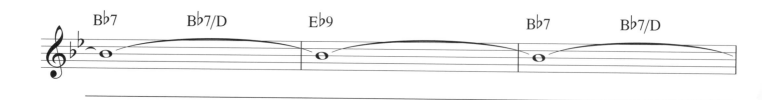

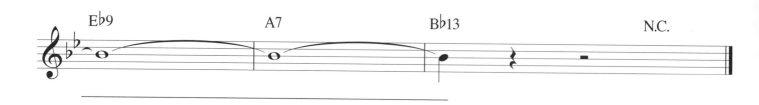

Do You Know the Way
to San Jose?

Lyric by Hal David
Music by Burt Bacharach

Intro
Brightly

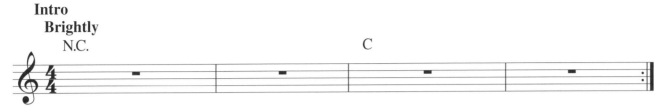

Verse

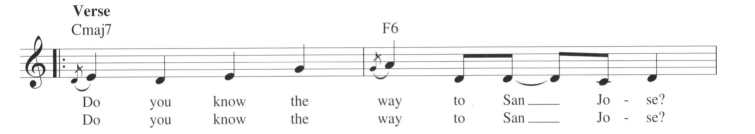

Do you know the way to San ___ Jo - se?
Do you know the way to San ___ Jo - se?

I've been a - way so long, I ___ may go
I'm go - in' back to find some ___ peace of

Bridge

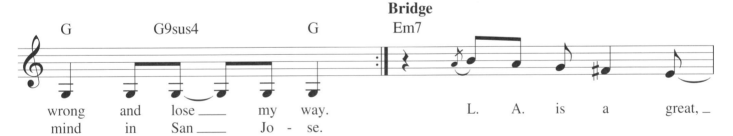

wrong and lose ___ my way. L. A. is a great, ___
mind in San ___ Jo - se.

___ big free - way, put a hun - dred down ___

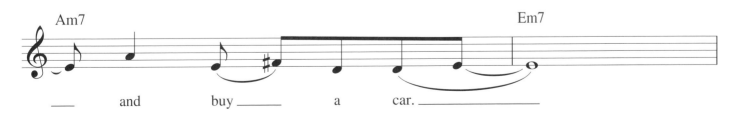

___ and buy ___ a car. ___

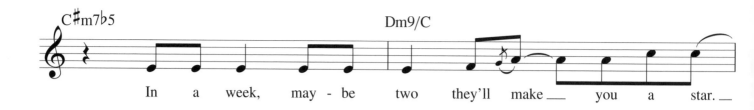

C#m7♭5 ... Dm9/C

In a week, may - be two they'll make ___ you a star. ___

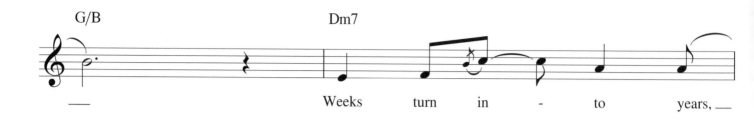

G/B ... Dm7

___ Weeks turn in - to years, ___

G

___ how quick ___ they pass. ___ And all those stars ___

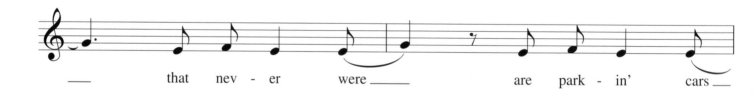

___ that nev - er were ___ are park - in' cars ___

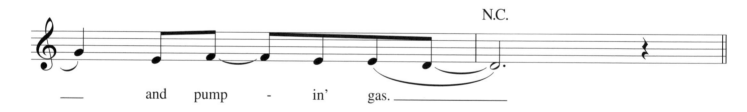

N.C.

___ and pump - in' gas. ___

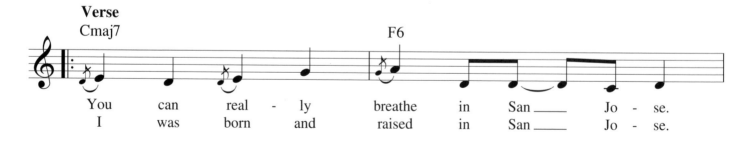

Verse

Cmaj7 ... F6

You can real - ly breathe in San ___ Jo - se.
I was born and raised in San ___ Jo - se.

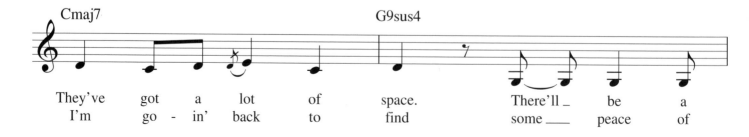

Cmaj7 ... G9sus4

They've got a lot of space. There'll _ be a
I'm go - in' back to find some ___ peace of

Bridge

23

and all the stars _____ that nev - er were _

_ are park - in' cars _____ and pump - in' gas. _____

N.C.

Verse
D♭maj7

I've got lots of
Do you know the

G♭6   D♭maj7

friends in San _____ Jo - se.
way to San _____ Jo - se?

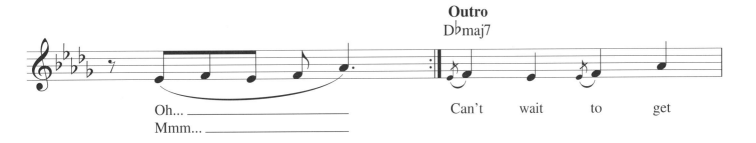

Outro
D♭maj7

Oh... _____
Mmm... _____

Can't wait to get

G♭6   D♭maj7

back to San _____ Jo - se.

D♭maj7   *Repeat and fade*

Fly Me to the Moon
(In Other Words)

Words and Music by Bart Howard

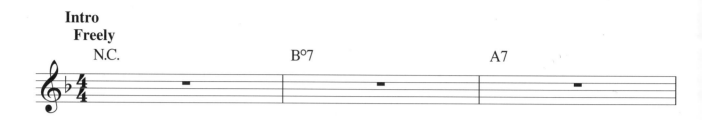

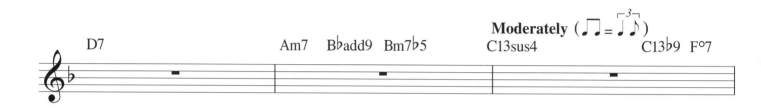

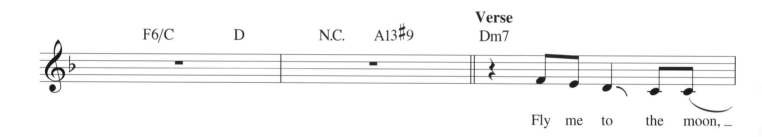

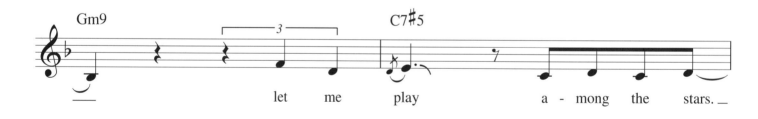

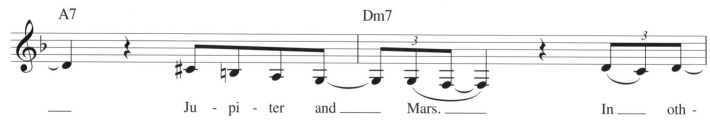

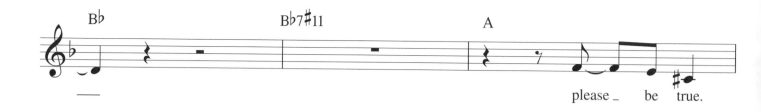

Bb   Bb7#11   A

please _ be true.

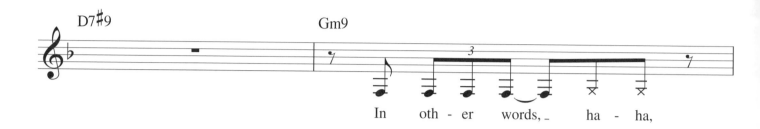

D7#9   Gm9

In oth-er words, _ ha-ha,

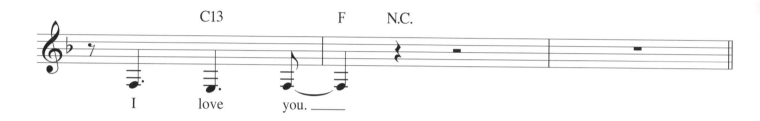

C13   F   N.C.

I love you. _____

Interlude

47

Verse

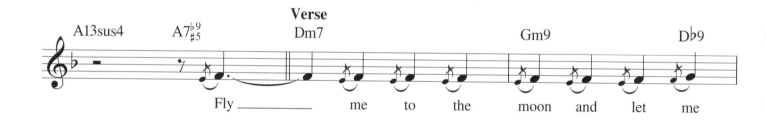

A13sus4   A7♭9#5   Dm7   Gm9   Db9

Fly _____ me to the moon and let me

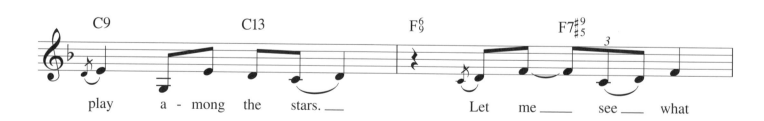

C9   C13   F6/9   F7#9#5

play a-mong the stars. ___ Let me ___ see ___ what

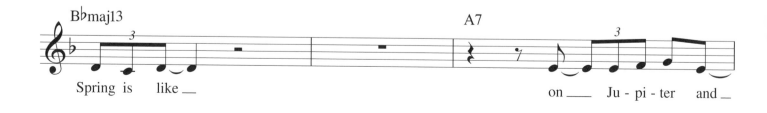

Bbmaj13   A7

Spring is like _   on ___ Ju-pi-ter and _

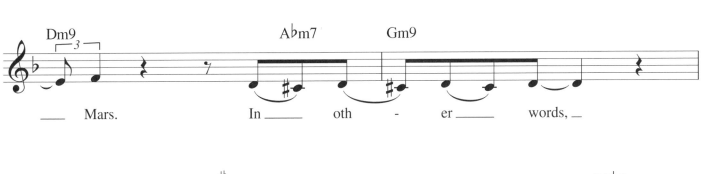

Mars.   In ___ oth - er ___ words, ___

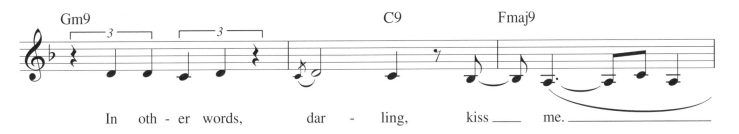

hold   my   hand. ___

In oth - er words,   dar - ling,   kiss ___ me. ___

Verse

___ Fill   my   life   with   song, ___   let me

sing   for - ev - er - more. ___   You ___

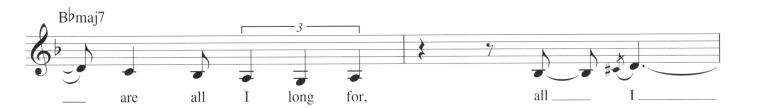

___ are   all   I   long   for,   all ___   I ___

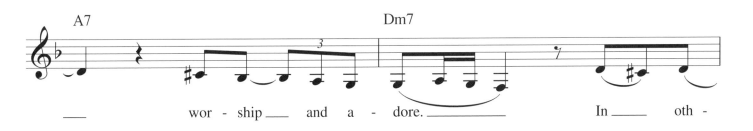

___   wor - ship ___ and a - dore. ___   In ___ oth -

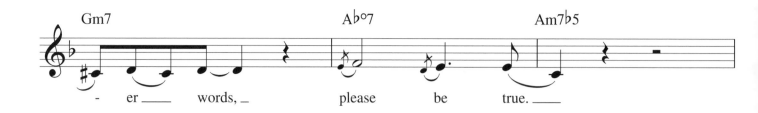

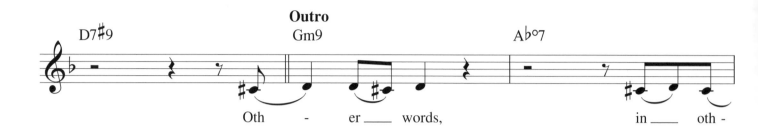

Outro

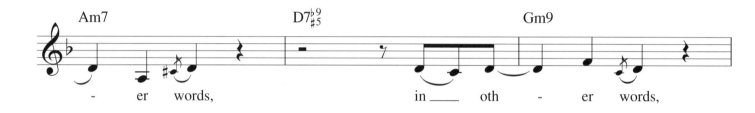

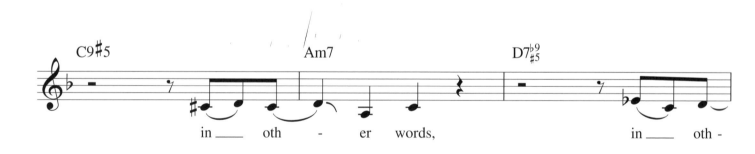

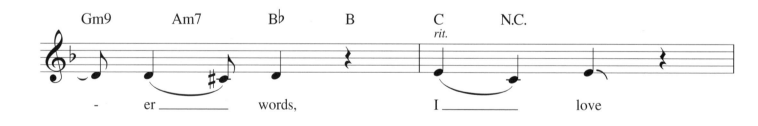

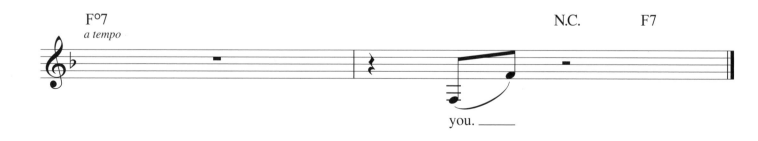

The Glory of Love

Words and Music by Billy Hill

How Deep Is the Ocean?
(How High Is the Sky)

Words and Music by Irving Berlin

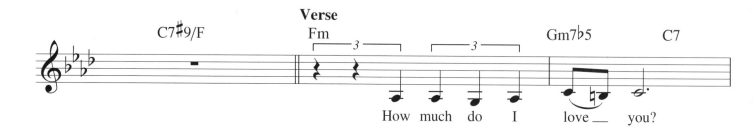

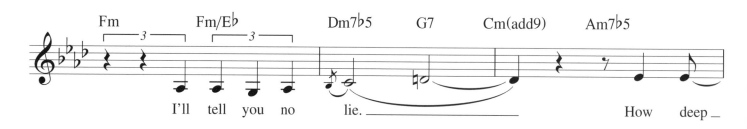

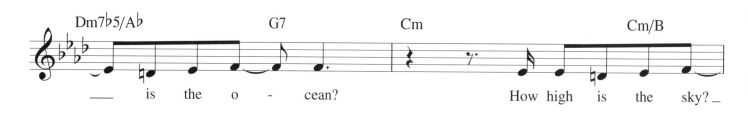

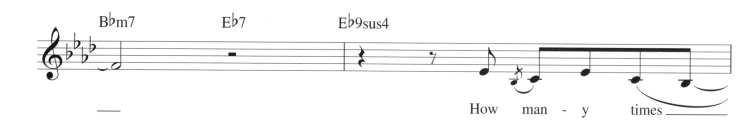

I'll Never Fall in Love Again

from PROMISES, PROMISES
Lyric by Hal David
Music by Burt Bacharach

Intro
Moderately

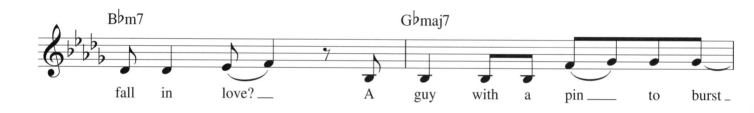

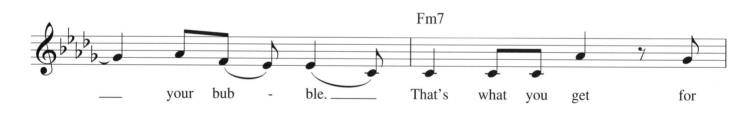

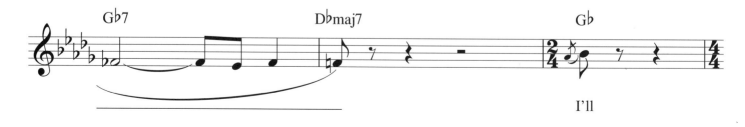

Bridge

Don't tell me what it's all _____ a - bout, _____

_____ 'cause I been there, and I'm glad I'm out. _____

Out of those ___ chains, those ___ chains that bind _____ you. ___

That is why I'm here to re - mind _____ you: _____

Verse

What do you get when you fall in love? ___ You

on - ly get lies and pain _____ and sor - row.

So, for at least un - til _____ to - mor - row, I'll _____

_____ nev - er fall in love a - gain. _____

40

No, — no, I'll

nev - er fall in love a - gain. —

Interlude-Bridge

Well, I'm out of those — chains, those —

chains that bind — you. — That is why I'm

Verse

here to re - mind — you: — What do you get when you

fall in love? — You on - ly get lies and pain —

— and sor - row. — So, for at least un -

Is You Is or Is You Ain't

(Ma' Baby)

from FOLLOW THE BOYS
from FIVE GUYS NAMED MOE
Words and Music by Billy Austin and Louis Jordan

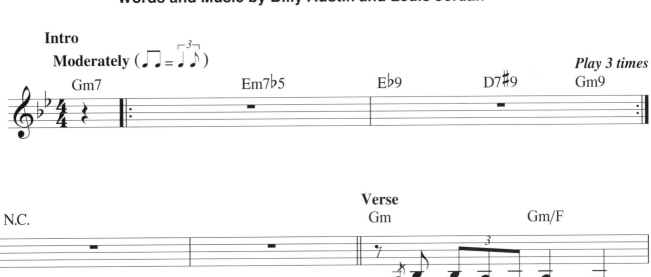

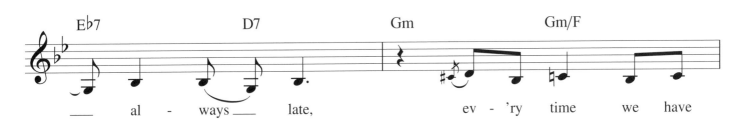

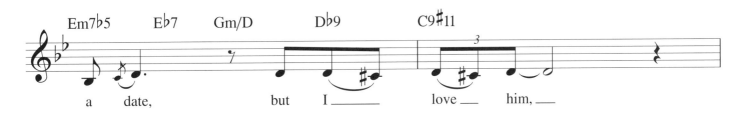

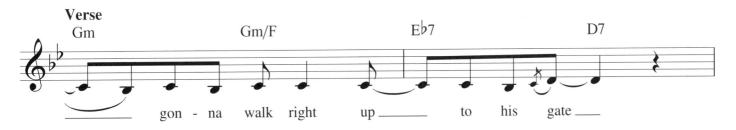

and see if I ____ can get it straight, 'cause __ I ____

want __ him, __ oh yes, ____ I'm ____ gon - na

Chorus

__ ask ___ him: _____ Is you is, or

is you ain't __ my __ ba - by?

The way you're act - in' late - ly makes me doubt. __

__ You have al - ways

been my _____ ba - by, ___ ba - by. ____

'Seems the flame in

Bridge

Chorus

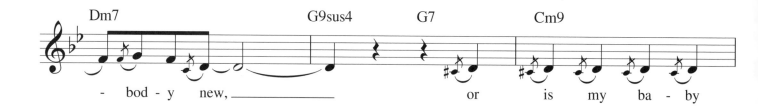

- bod - y new, _____ or is my ba - by

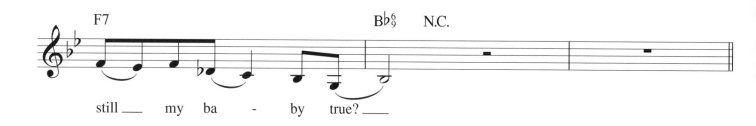

still __ my ba - by true? ___

Interlude (Saxophone)

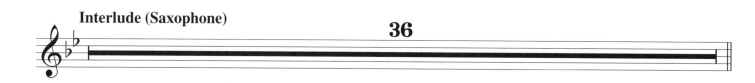

36

Interlude (Piano)

16

Bridge

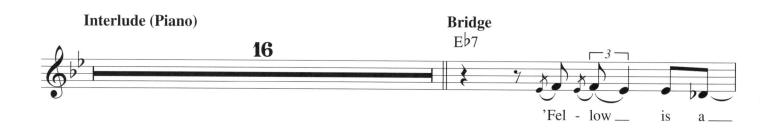

'Fel - low __ is a ___

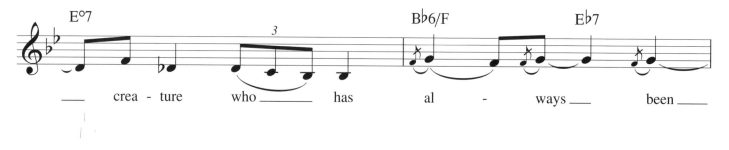

__ crea - ture who _____ has al - ways __ been ___

__ strange. Just when you think you're his, ___

__ you know he's gone _____ and made __

Let's Face the Music and Dance

from the Motion Picture FOLLOW THE FLEET
Words and Music by Irving Berlin

Intro
Bossa Nova

Verse

There __ may be ___ trou - ble a - head,

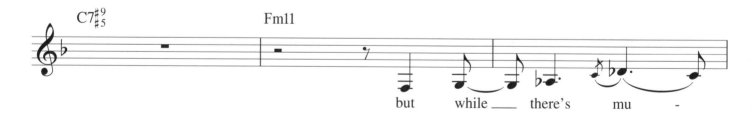

but while ___ there's mu -

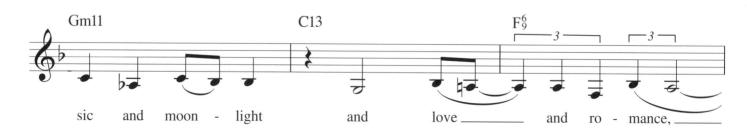

sic and moon - light and love ___ and ro - mance, ___

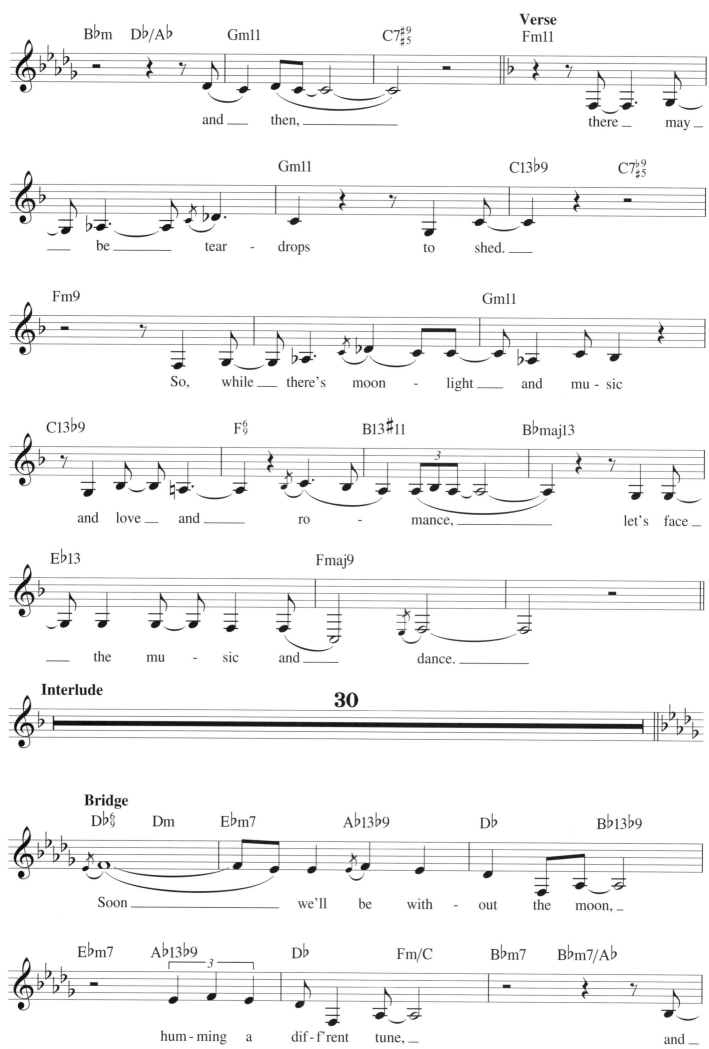

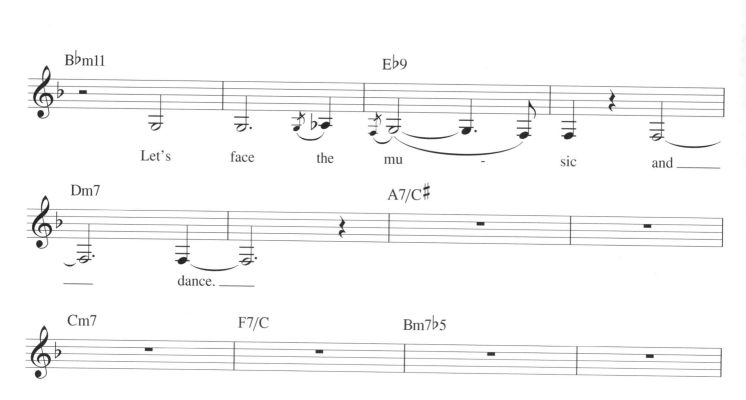

Let's face the mu - sic and ___ dance. ___

Let's face the ___ mu - sic and ___ dance. ___

Let's face the mu - sic and dance.

Pick Yourself Up

from SWING TIME
Words by Dorothy Fields
Music by Jerome Kern

Interlude (Guitar)

8

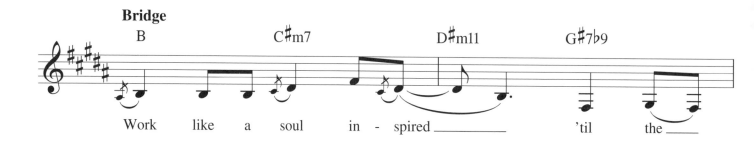

Bridge

B   C#m7   D#m11   G#7♭9

Work   like   a   soul   in - spired _____ 'til   the _____

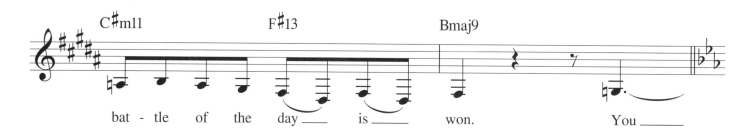

C#m11   F#13   Bmaj9

bat - tle   of   the   day ___ is ___ won.   You ____

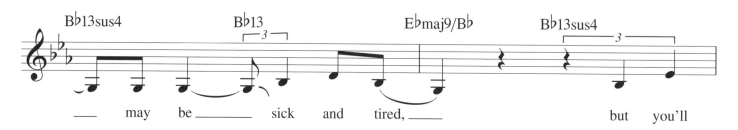

B♭13sus4   B♭13   E♭maj9/B♭   B♭13sus4

__ may   be ___ sick   and   tired, ____ but   you'll

Fm9   B♭m11   Cm7   F7♭9

be ___ a   man, ___ my ___ son.   Don't __

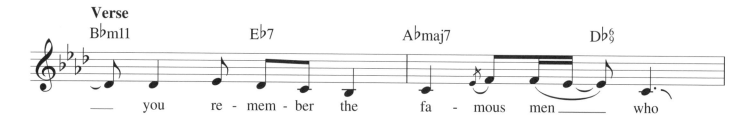

Verse

B♭m11   E♭7   A♭maj7   D♭⁶⁄₉

__ you   re - mem - ber   the   fa - mous   men ___ who

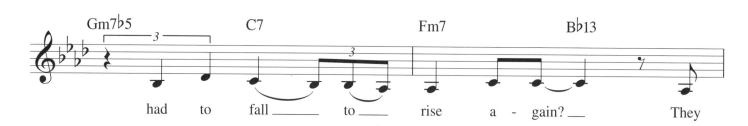

Gm7♭5   C7   Fm7   B♭13

had   to   fall ___ to ___ rise   a - gain? ___ They

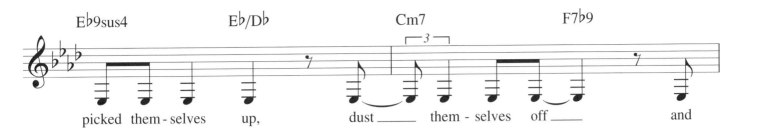

picked them-selves up, dust _____ them-selves off _____ and

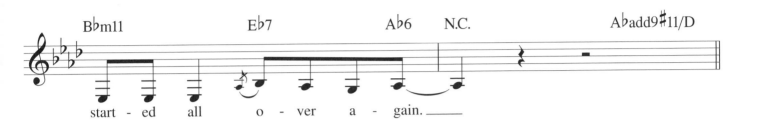

start - ed all o - ver a - gain. _____

Outro

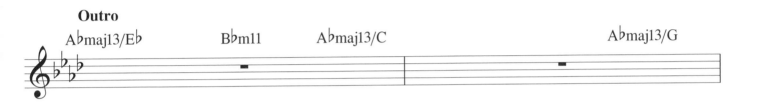

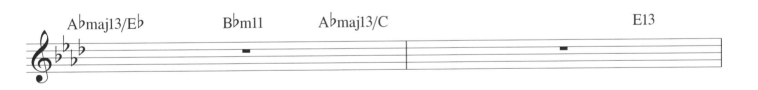

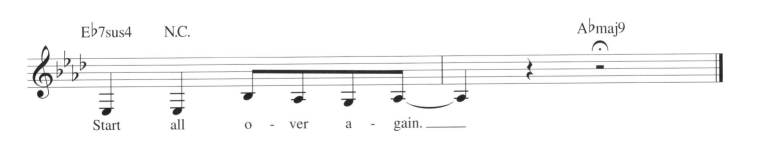

Start all o - ver a - gain. _____

Puttin' On the Ritz

from the Motion Picture PUTTIN' ON THE RITZ
Words and Music by Irving Berlin

Intro
Moderately

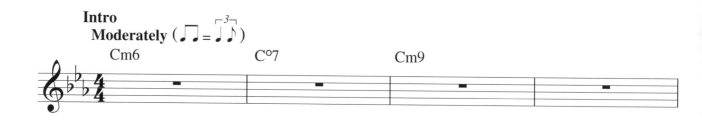

Verse

If you're blue and you ____ don't know where to

go to, why don't you go where fash - ion sits?

Put - tin' on ____ the Ritz.

Verse

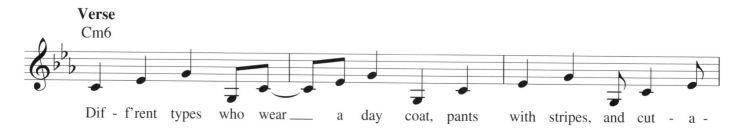

Dif - f'rent types who wear ____ a day coat, pants with stripes, and cut - a-

Shout

Words and Music by O'Kelly Isley, Ronald Isley and Rudolph Isley

Intro
Brightly, double-time feel

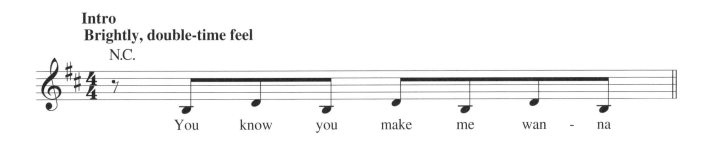

You know you make me wan - na

Chorus

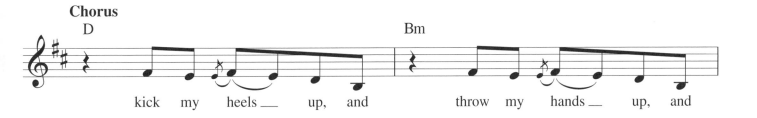

kick my heels _ up, and   throw my hands _ up, and

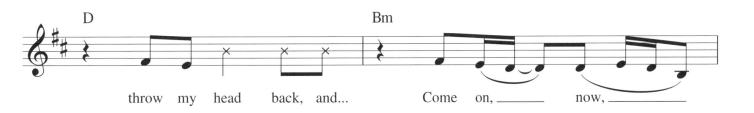

throw my head back, and...   Come on, _____ now, _____

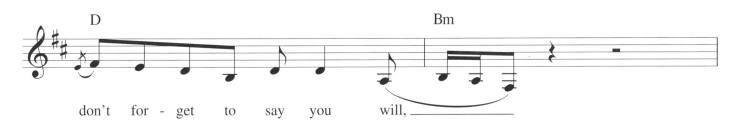

don't for - get to say you   will, _____

don't for - get to say yeah,   yeah, _ yeah,   yeah, _ yeah. _

Say it right now, ba - by.

sis - ters, _____ a - much __ bet - ter than I been to my - self,

so good, __ so good, and if a - you ev - er leave __

_____ me, _____ I don't want no - bod - y else,

hey, ___ hey. _____ I said I want you to know, __

_____ I said I want you to know __

(♫ = ♫)

N.C.

___ right now. _____ You know you make me wan - na

Chorus
Double-time feel

E   C#m

kick my heels __ up, and   throw my hands __ up, and

E   C#m

throw my head __ back, and   come on, _____ now, _____

64

come on, _____ now, _____   come on, _____ now, _____

come on, _____ now. _____   Play it, Sis - ter Al - len, hey!

Instrumental

18

Interlude

Hey. _____

Well, hey, _____ yeah.

A lit - tle bit soft - er, now. _____   A lit - tle bit soft - er now. _____

A lit - tle bit soft - er, now. _   A lit - tle bit soft - er, now. _

Ver - y qui - et, girls. _____   Take it eas - y.

A lit-tle bit soft-er, now. ___ A lit-tle bit soft-er.

A lit-tle bit loud-er, now. ___ A lit-tle bit loud-er, now.

A lit-tle bit loud-er, now. ___ A lit-tle bit loud-er, now. ___

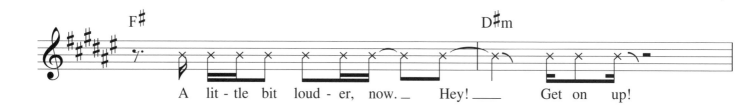

A lit-tle bit loud-er, now. ___ Hey! ___ Get on up!

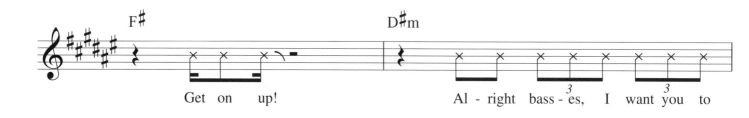

Get on up! Al-right bass-es, I want you to

do it.

Come on, ___ now. ___

Come on, ___ now. ___ Come on, girls.

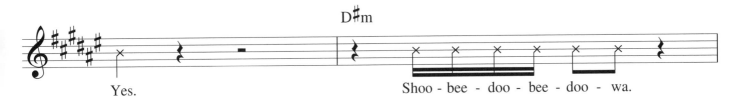

Yes. Shoo - bee - doo - bee - doo - wa.

Hey! Here I come. Shout!

Shout! Shout! Shout!

Shout! Hoo! ___ Shout! Shout!

Shout! Woo! ___ Hey. ___

___ Hoo! ___ Hey. ___

Chorus

Kick my heels __ up, and throw my hands __ up, and

throw my head __ back, and come on, __ now, __

say it, Mad __ Rob - in. Come on, __ come on.

Yeah, _____ yeah!

Say it right __ now, ba - by.

Well, come on, __ come on, _____ yeah. __

Say that you will. _____ *(Spoken:) Now, wait a minute.*

Outro

N.C.
a tempo

Alright, who was that?

Skylark

Words by Johnny Mercer
Music by Hoagy Carmichael

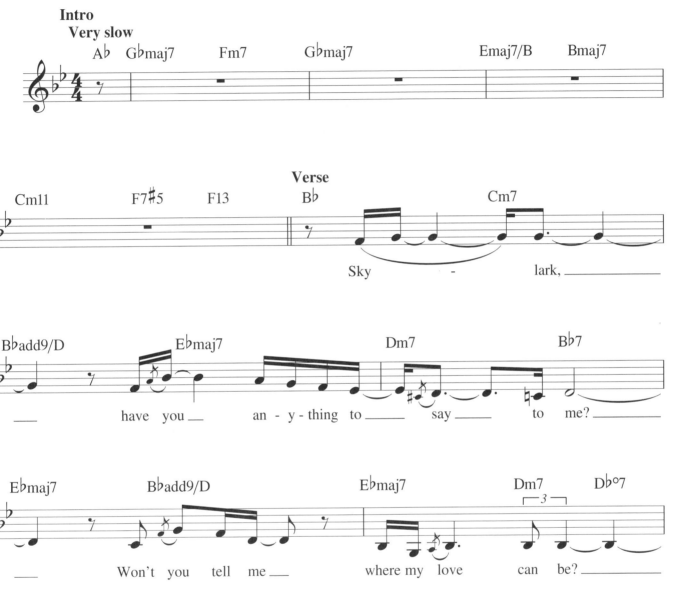

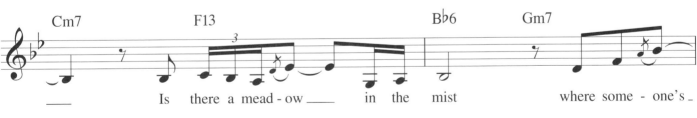

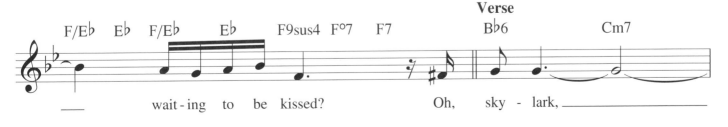

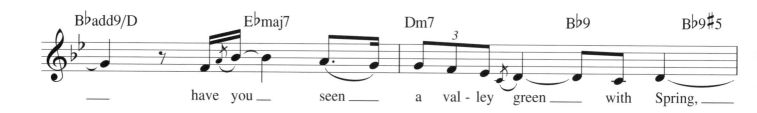

have you __ seen __ a val-ley green __ with Spring, __

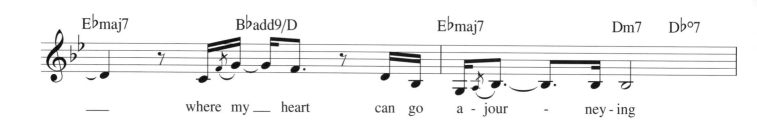

__ where my __ heart can go a-jour - ney-ing

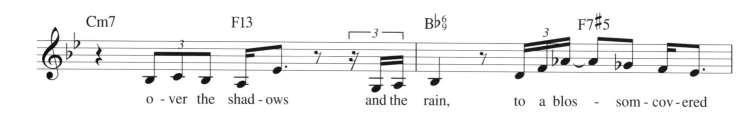

o - ver the shad-ows and the rain, to a blos - som-cov-ered

Bridge

lane? And __ in your lone - ly flight,

have - n't you heard __ the mu - sic in _____ the night?

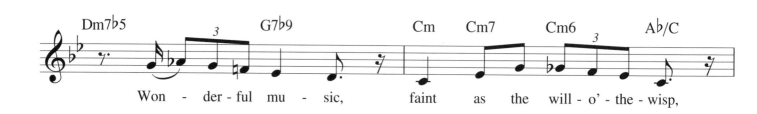

Won - der-ful mu - sic, faint as the will - o' - the - wisp,

cra - zy __ as a loon, _____ sad as a gyp-sy ser -

70

e - nad - ing the moon. Oh, ___ sky - lark, ___

___ I don't _ know _ if you can find ___ these _ things, ___

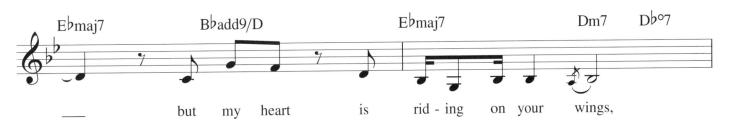

___ but my heart is rid - ing on your wings,

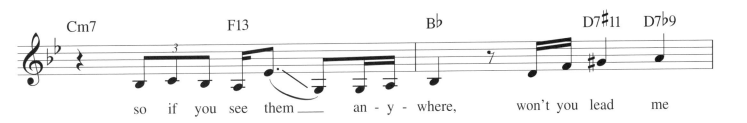

so if you see them ___ an - y - where, won't you lead me

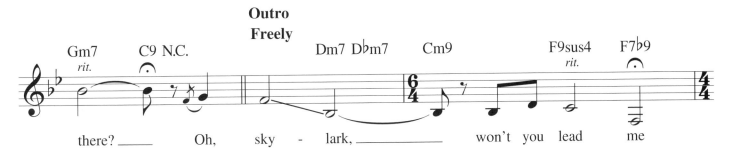

there? ___ Oh, sky - lark, ___ won't you lead me

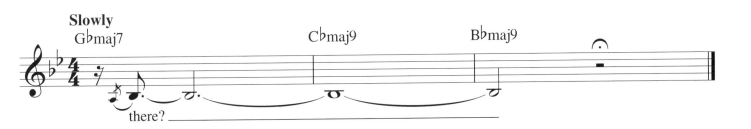

there? ___

Snowbird

Words and Music by Gene MacLellan

When You Wish Upon a Star

Words by Ned Washington
Music by Leigh Harline

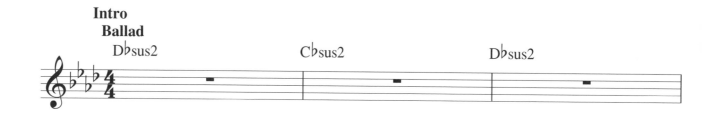

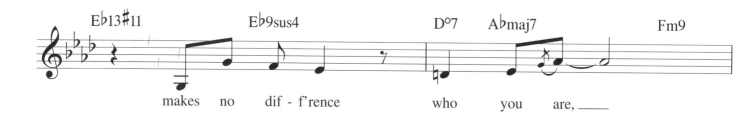

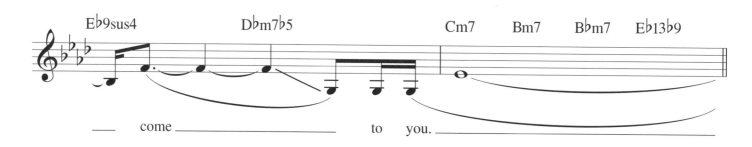

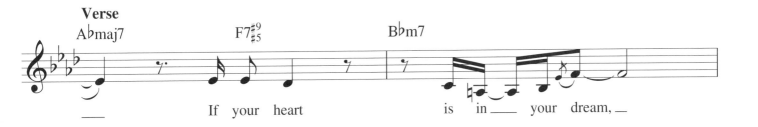

Verse

If your heart is in your dream,

no re-quest is too ex-treme,

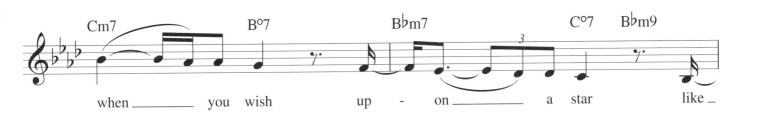

when you wish up-on a star like

Bridge

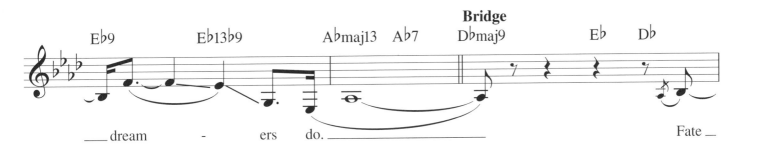

dreamers do. Fate

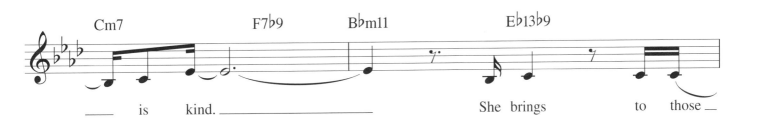

is kind. She brings to those

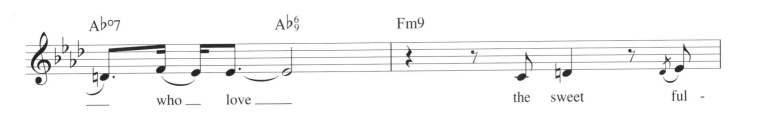

who love the sweet ful-

Verse

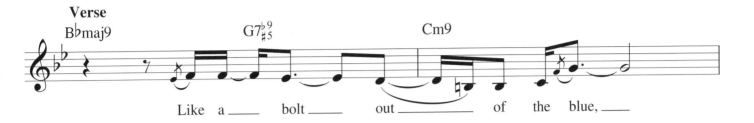

Like a ___ bolt ___ out ___ of the blue, ___

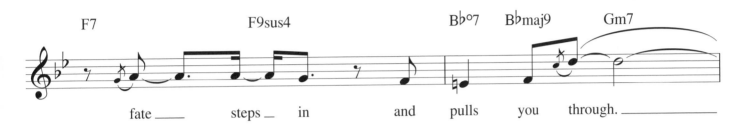

fate ___ steps ___ in and pulls you through. ___

___ When ___ you wish ___ up - on a star, your

Outro

dream comes

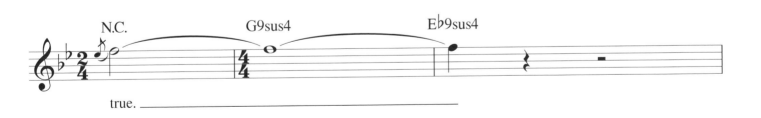

true. ___

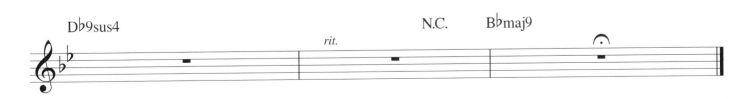

Pro Vocal® Series

SONGBOOK & SOUND-ALIKE CD
SING 8 GREAT SONGS
WITH A PROFESSIONAL BAND

Whether you're a karaoke singer or an auditioning professional, the Pro Vocal® series is for you! Unlike most karaoke packs, each book in the Pro Vocal Series contains the lyrics, melody, and chord symbols for eight hit songs. The CD contains demos for listening, and separate backing tracks so you can sing along. The CD is playable on any CD player, but it is also enhanced so PC and Mac computer users can adjust the recording to any pitch without changing the tempo! Perfect for home rehearsal, parties, auditions, corporate events, and gigs without a backup band.

WOMEN'S EDITIONS

00740409	**1. Broadway Standards**	$14.95
00740249	**2. Jazz Standards**	$14.95
00740246	**3. Contemporary Hits**	$14.95
00740277	**4. '80s Gold**	$12.95
00740299	**5. Christmas Standards**	$15.95
00740281	**6. Disco Fever**	$12.95
00740279	**7. R&B Super Hits**	$12.95
00740309	**8. Wedding Gems**	$12.95
00740409	**9. Broadway Standards**	$14.95
00740348	**10. Andrew Lloyd Webber**	$14.95
00740344	**11. Disney's Best**	$14.99
00740378	**12. Ella Fitzgerald**	$14.95
00740350	**14. Musicals of Boublil & Schönberg**	$14.95
00740377	**15. Kelly Clarkson**	$14.95
00740342	**16. Disney Favorites**	$14.95
00740353	**17. Jazz Ballads**	$12.95
00740376	**18. Jazz Vocal Standards**	$14.95
00740375	**20. Hannah Montana**	$16.95
00740354	**21. Jazz Favorites**	$14.99
00740374	**22. Patsy Cline**	$14.95
00740369	**23. Grease**	$14.95
00740367	**25. ABBA**	$14.95
00740365	**26. Movie Songs**	$14.95
00740360	**28. High School Musical 1 & 2**	$14.95
00740363	**29. Torch Songs**	$14.99
00740379	**30. Hairspray**	$14.95
00740380	**31. Top Hits**	$14.95
00740384	**32. Hits of the '70s**	$14.95
00740388	**33. Billie Holiday**	$14.95
00740389	**34. The Sound of Music**	$15.99
00740390	**35. Contemporary Christian**	$14.95
00740392	**36. Wicked**	$15.99
00740393	**37. More Hannah Montana**	$14.95
00740394	**38. Miley Cyrus**	$14.95
00740396	**39. Christmas Hits**	$15.95
00740410	**40. Broadway Classics**	$14.95
00740415	**41. Broadway Favorites**	$14.99
00740416	**42. Great Standards You Can Sing**	$14.99
00740417	**43. Singable Standards**	$14.99
00740418	**44. Favorite Standards**	$14.99
00740419	**45. Sing Broadway**	$14.99
00740420	**46. More Standards**	$14.99
00740421	**47. Timeless Hits**	$14.99
00740422	**48. Easygoing R&B**	$14.99

MEN'S EDITIONS

00740248	**1. Broadway Songs**	$14.95
00740250	**2. Jazz Standards**	$14.95
00740251	**3. Contemporary Hits**	$14.99
00740278	**4. '80s Gold**	$12.95
00740298	**5. Christmas Standards**	$15.95
00740280	**6. R&B Super Hits**	$12.95
00740282	**7. Disco Fever**	$12.95
00740310	**8. Wedding Gems**	$12.95
00740411	**9. Broadway Greats**	$14.99
00740333	**10. Elvis Presley – Volume 1**	$14.95
00740349	**11. Andrew Lloyd Webber**	$14.95
00740345	**12. Disney's Best**	$14.95
00740347	**13. Frank Sinatra Classics**	$14.95
00740334	**14. Lennon & McCartney**	$14.99
00740335	**16. Elvis Presley – Volume 2**	$14.99
00740343	**17. Disney Favorites**	$14.95
00740351	**18. Musicals of Boublil & Schönberg**	$14.95
00740346	**20. Frank Sinatra Standards**	$14.95
00740362	**27. Michael Bublé**	$14.95
00740361	**28. High School Musical 1 & 2**	$14.95
00740364	**29. Torch Songs**	$14.95
00740366	**30. Movie Songs**	$14.95
00740368	**31. Hip Hop Hits**	$14.95
00740370	**32. Grease**	$14.95
00740371	**33. Josh Groban**	$14.95
00740373	**34. Billy Joel**	$17.99
00740381	**35. Hits of the '50s**	$14.95
00740382	**36. Hits of the '60s**	$14.95
00740383	**37. Hits of the '70s**	$14.95
00740385	**38. Motown**	$14.95
00740386	**39. Hank Williams**	$14.95
00740387	**40. Neil Diamond**	$14.99
00740391	**41. Contemporary Christian**	$14.95
00740397	**42. Christmas Hits**	$15.95
00740399	**43. Ray**	$14.95
00740400	**44. The Rat Pack Hits**	$14.99
00740401	**45. Songs in the Style of Nat "King" Cole**	$14.99
00740402	**46. At the Lounge**	$14.95
00740403	**47. The Big Band Singer**	$14.95
00740404	**48. Jazz Cabaret Songs**	$14.99
00740405	**49. Cabaret Songs**	$14.99
00740406	**50. Big Band Standards**	$14.99
00740412	**51. Broadway's Best**	$14.99
00740427	**52. Great Standards Collection**	$19.99

MIXED EDITIONS

These editions feature songs for both male and female voices.

00740311	**1. Wedding Duets**	$12.95
00740398	**2. Enchanted**	$14.95
00740407	**3. Rent**	$14.95
00740408	**4. Broadway Favorites**	$14.99
00740413	**5. South Pacific**	$15.99
00740414	**6. High School Musical 3**	$14.99

FOR MORE INFORMATION, SEE YOUR LOCAL MUSIC DEALER,
OR WRITE TO:

HAL•LEONARD®
CORPORATION
7777 W. BLUEMOUND RD. P.O. BOX 13819 MILWAUKEE, WI 53213

Visit Hal Leonard online at www.halleonard.com

0509